WHEAT BELLY

21 DAY WHEAT-FREE MEAL PLAN, FULL OF QUICK AND NUTRITIOUS RECIPES

CHARLOTTE MOYER

Copyright © 2015 - All Rights Reserved - Invicta House Publishing

**Receive my next book for free!
Exclusive promotions, updates and newsletters**
Join my **Book Club Now**

Copyright: All rights reserved. No part of this publication may be reproduced or transmitted in any form whatsoever, electronic, or mechanical, including photocopying, recording, or by any informational storage or retrieval system without express written, dated and signed permission from the author.

Table of Contents

Welcome

Introduction

The Basics of the Wheat Belly Diet

Wheat-Belly Breakfast Recipes

    Strawberry Smoothie

    Asparagus & Eggs

    Orange & Date Salad

    Scrambled Eggs

    Egg Pots

    Exotic Breakfast Smoothie

    Fruit Salad

Wheat Belly Lunch Recipes

    Oriental Salad

    Parmesan Salad

    Nutty hummus

    Greek Feta Salad

    Pesto Salad

    Prawn Lunch

    Vegetable Soup

Wheat Belly Main Course Recipes

- Hearty Mediterranean Stew
- Filled Eggplants
- Fish Broth
- Mediterranean Grilled Chicken
- Spiced Salmon with corn salad
- Ginger Stir-Fry

The 21 Day Meal Plan

- Week 1
- Week 2
- Week 3

Complete Food List

Conclusion

Other Books By Author

- Wheat Belly: 31 Delicious Wheat Free Recipes to Lose Weight Fast
- Vegan: 35 High Protein Vegan Recipes for Weight Loss and Building Muscle
- How to Bake Perfectly: 101 Tips, Tricks & Cheats for Baking Recipes
- How to Make Money from Home: 7 Steps to Make Money from Baking recipes

Welcome

Thank you for purchasing this, *'Wheat Belly: 21 Day Wheat-Free Meal Plan, Full of Quick & Nutritious Recipes'*. This eBook aims to inform you about the new and effective wheat belly diet that advocates an avoidance of wheat, wheat-based products and a few other grains and carbohydrates. This eBook guides you to avoid the advantages of the wheat belly diet, provides wheat belly recipes for breakfast, lunch and dinner as well as providing you with a meal plan to get started on your new diet.

Let's get started!

Charlotte Moyer

PS…Don't forget to join my [Book Club](#)

Introduction

The wheat belly diet follows a simple premise: abandon all sources of wheat from your diet and lose weight. This new diet is gaining a huge amount of popularity throughout the Western world. Unlike other diets which promote harsh and difficult calorie counting techniques or fad diets which require bizarre and potentially dangerous eating patterns, the wheat diet is safe and easy.

Once you find a few substitutes for the wheat foods you probably eat everyday – pasta, bread, cereal and baked goods – you can stick and maintain the diet almost without thought. The little effort you need to get started will be diminished by this eBook which provides you with a 21-day meal plan and a bundle of wheat-free recipes to kick start your new diet.

This eBook contains five chapters. The first chapter details why you need to try the wheat belly diet – not only for weight loss, but also for its various other health-related benefits.

The second, third and fourth chapter provides a few recipes for each breakfast, lunch and dinner respectively, demonstrating the kind of foods and dishes you can expect to eat on this new diet.

Lastly, all the information of the previous three chapters is compiled in the fifth chapter, which details a 21-day meal plan for your convenience.

If you've always wanted to shed the pounds and have become disillusioned with tiresome calorie counting or 'the latest super-food' than give the wheat-belly diet a try. Your waistline will thank you.

The Basics of the Wheat Belly Diet

Although the term 'diet' is used, the wheat belly diet is unlike anything you will have tried before. You don't need to restrict your intake of foods and you do not even need to limit yourself to eating predominantly one or two types of food. In the wheat belly 'diet' you can eat almost anything you want, whenever you want – with just the one rule that you avoid wheat.

So you may be asking, why wheat? There have been so many targets and scapegoats for obesity in the past few decades; fats, saturates, salt, sugar, calories and so on. Why is wheat the latest target on the scientific firing grounds? The truth is that research is starting to reveal that wheat may be unhealthy for you in multiple ways.

The first reason that wheat is unhealthy for you is its effect on your blood sugar levels. Consistently high blood sugar levels can lead to various medical complications (such as type 2 diabetes) whilst low sugar levels can lead to a lack of energy and sluggishness. Ideally, you want the level of sugar in your blood to be relatively stable and increase or decrease gradually over the day as you consume food and expend energy.

However, wheat may compromise the balance of your sugar levels. The theory behind the wheat belly diet advocates that wheat and the carbohydrates it contains are too easily digested and broken down by the body in glucose. Hence, when wheat-based products are eaten blood sugar spikes, in a similar fashion to the way foods high in sugar cause your body's blood sugar to rocket. This is not only detrimental as high blood sugar can be dangerous to your health in the long term, but it also causes energy lows as your blood sugar levels crash over time. Other non-wheat carbohydrates are broken and digested slower which causes the sugars in those carbohydrates to be absorbed by the blood more gradually. When eating other carbohydrates, blood sugar levels do not peak as high, but they stay more stable and decrease slower.

It is important to note that this pattern of harmful blood sugar levels its suggested for both white grains and also brown grains. Many contemporary diets and meal plans would argue that brown bead and more complex carbohydrates do not cause such spikes in your blood sugar – however, the wheat belly diet thinks differently. The proof, ironically, is in the pudding; thousands of people are experiencing the weight loss effects and increased energy levels of the wheat belly diet. There is no smoke without fire.

As before mentioned, stable and consistent blood sugar levels lead to increased energy and vigor throughout the day. If you find yourself needing coffee or other stimulants to keep yourself going an hour or two after your breakfast, you may be struggling with post-meal sugar lows. The wheat-belly diet can help. Similarly, if you find yourself tired all the time, perhaps it is not a lack of sleep or various psychological factors that are causing your ailment – it may be an excess of wheat in your diet.

In addition to the effect of wheat on your blood sugar and energy levels, not eating wheat in your diet is suggested to reduce bloating. If, after meals you find your stomach and chest uncomfortable with the sensation of food it may be the wheat you have eaten that is culpable. Furthermore, many individuals find that their entire digestive systems go into chaos when they eat wheat, causing symptoms such as constipation, diarrhea or stomach cramps.

If you experience any digestive problems after eating wheat, you may be suffering from wheat sensitivity or a more serious digestive disease.

There exists a body of people in the population who are diagnosed with various wheat-related health problems such as celiac disease or wheat allergy.

In the former case, individuals with celiac disease cannot absorb the gluten – a protein – from wheat (as well as other foods). The immune system of people with celiac disease attacks the tissues in the small intestine – where food is digested and absorbed into the body. This damages these tissues preventing various nutrients from entering the body of people with celiac disease. Celiac disease can lead to a wide range of health issues due to the inflammation of the bowels, a failure to absorb nutrition from the body as well the body's immune system becoming compromised. It is believed that around 1 in 100 people suffer from some form of celiac disease.

In the case of wheat allergies, the body's own immune system also starts attacking the cells in the body when wheat is eaten, as if the wheat were a pathogen that needed to be destroyed. Unlike celiac disease however, the symptoms associated with wheat allergy are more consistent with the symptoms of other allergies – such as sneezing, itching and watery eyes.

If you suspect you have a wheat allergy or celiac disease it is important to visit your local doctor or general practitioner. These individuals may able to prevent you from suffering with long-term complications.

However, wheat sensitivity is more subtle. Wheat sensitivity is harder to diagnose than wheat allergies or celiac disease and its symptoms, although uncomfortable, are less dire. Ultimately, the only way for you to test whether you have wheat sensitivity or not is to go on a wheat elimination diet – the wheat belly diet – for several weeks and see if your digestive system feels better. You might also lose some weight – killing two birds with one stone.

In addition to all these former mentioned effects, there is some evidence to suggest that wheat may be addictive. Some scientists advocate that certain proteins in wheat can be broken down by the small intestine into chemicals that elicit your body to release endorphins – neurotransmitters in your brain responsible for feelings of pleasure. The consequence of this is that you feel good when you eat wheat and achieve a small 'high'. This not only causes your appetite to increase, but subtly and sub-consciously increases your desire to consume wheat again. You become addicted.

Now that you understand the advantages of a wheat-belly diet, it is time to get into the facts and details of what you cannot eat. You must avoid entirely, or eat very, very rarely foods that contain wheat. This includes the following types of food:

Bread

Couscous

Pasta

Cereals

Pasties

Cakes

Doughnuts

Most Baked Goods

Beer

Soy Sauce

In addition to avoiding these foods, it is also strongly recommended that you avoid starchy foods such as white rice, brown rice and potatoes. These foods are believed to cause similar effects on the bodies sugar levels as wheat – with all the detrimental health effects these blood sugar levels entail.

On top of this it is actually suggested that you also avoid gluten-free foods. This may sound counter-intuitive, but gluten-free products go against the ethos of the wheat-belly diet as they often contain substances that are harmful to blood sugar levels, such as processed corn starch.

Do not be deceived, it may seem as though gluten-free products follow the same principle as wheat-free products, but this couldn't be further from the truth. However, with that being said, be aware of the distinction between gluten-free products and gluten-free meals. Gluten-free meals are typically fine – it is the processed gluten-free goods which are harmful.

Finally, you are also instructed to avoid foods which are especially high in sugar, such as candies and ice-cream.

Whilst this may seem a little restrictive, the wheat belly diet recommends a whole range of alternate, healthier foods to promote wellbeing.

These include, but are not limited to:

Fish

Foul

Meat

Nuts

Eggs

Seeds

Olive Oil

Coconut Oil

Walnut Oil

Avocadoes

Fruit

Vegetables

If you need to use flour for a recipe, replace wheat flour with a healthier substitute. Almond flour, coconut flour or various seed meals make great alternatives.

To conclude this chapter, the essence of the wheat belly diet is avoiding foods, such as wheat, grains and various other carbohydrates that cause blood sugar levels to spike. Increased blood sugar levels lead to health complications and also a lack of energy when these sugar levels eventually crash. Furthermore wheat may also be addictive and responsible for various digestive issues such as cramps or constipation.

WHEAT-BELLY BREAKFAST RECIPES

STRAWBERRY SMOOTHIE

Total Preparation Time:

Approx 5 minutes

Ingredients (serves two):

½ avocado

150g strawberries

4 tablespoons low-fat natural yogurt

Lemon juice

Honey

Nutritional Information:

200 calories

9g protein

15g carbohydrates

11g fat

3g saturates

3g fiber

15g sugar

0.3g salt

Procedure:

Stone the avocado and remove the flesh. Combine the avocado, strawberries and natural yogurt with a little honey and lemon juice with a tablespoon of water. Process in blender until thoroughly liquidized.

Asparagus & Eggs

Total Preparation Time:

Approx 20 minutes

Ingredients (serves four):

1 tablespoon olive oil

A pinch of chili

A pinch of paprika

20 asparagus spears

4 medium eggs

Nutritional Information:

190 calories

12g protein

12g carbohydrates

10g fat

2g saturates

2g fiber

3g sugar

0.72g salt

Procedure:

In a frying pan, heat the olive oil. Add the asparagus and coat with the chili and paprika and a little salt, frying for a minute on each side.

Remove the asparagus spear from the frying pan and add them to a saucepan of boiling water for 3 minutes.

Whilst the asparagus is boiling, add eggs to the boiling water, also boiling for around 3 minutes. Drain the eggs and asparagus from the water, placing each egg in an egg cup. Serve each egg with several asparagus spears to dip in the egg yolk.

Orange & Date Salad

Total Preparation Time:

Approx 15 minutes

Ingredients (serves four):

4 oranges

12 dates

Fresh mint leaves

1 tablespoon of rose syrup

Nutritional Information:

220 calories

4g protein

54 carbohydrates

1g fat

0g saturates

5g fiber

54g sugar

>0.05g salt

Procedure:

Stone the dates and chop them into large chunks. Peel the oranges and slice them into eight pieces, ensuring no pith remains. Chop the mint leaves finely. Add the oranges to the dates and cover with mint and rose syrup. Separate into four portions and serve.

SCRAMBLED EGGS

Total Preparation Time:

Approx 20 minutes

Ingredients (serves four):

2 tablespoons of single cream

2 large eggs

A knob of butter

Nutritional Information:

254 calories

18g protein

4g carbohydrates

19g fat

7g saturates

0g fiber

0g sugar

0.6g salt

Procedure:

Combine the eggs, cream and a little salt in a bowl, until there is a single mixture. Heat the butter on a frying pan, ensuring that the butter melts and greases the ban but does not discolor and become brown.

Pour the egg mixture onto the frying pan and allow the mixture to rest and set for 30 seconds. Next, using a wooden spoon mix and raise the egg mixture and leave it to set for 15 seconds. Repeat this process until the eggs are solidified or chunky.

Egg Pots

Total Preparation Time:

Approx 20 minutes

Ingredients (serves four):

100g spinach

400g chopped tomatoes

1teaspon chili

4 medium eggs

Nutritional Information:

114 calories

9g protein

3g carbohydrates

7g fat

2g saturates

2g fiber

2g sugar

0.5g salt

Procedure:

Preheat the oven to gas mark 6 or 400 degrees F. Cut the spinach into fine pieces and separate between four baking dishes. Add the chopped tomatoes with the chili powder and then pour over the spinach. Dig a small ditch in the center of the tomatoes in each dish and crack and egg into the ditch. Cook in the oven for 15 minutes. Serve with salad or a savory side.

Exotic Breakfast Smoothie

<u>Total Preparation Time:</u>

Approx 5 minutes

<u>Ingredients (serves two):</u>

1 mango

400ml skimmed milk

½ cup natural yogurt

2 tablespoons almond meal

1 tablespoon of honey

Ice

<u>Nutritional Information:</u>

265 calories

15g protein

35g carbohydrates

7.5g fat

0.5g saturates

2.5g fiber

33g sugar

>0.05g salt

<u>Procedure:</u>

Peel the mango and dice it into small chunks. Combine the mango, milk, almond, honey and yogurt in a food processor with some ice. Process until the mixture is smooth and consistent.

Separate into two servings and serve.

Fruit Salad

Total Preparation Time:

Approx 10 minutes

Ingredients (serves four):

250g strawberries

2 bananas

2 oranges

1 apple

200g light Greek yogurt

1 tablespoon of honey

1/3 cup almonds

Nutritional Information:

250 calories

8g protein

31g carbohydrates

8.5g fat

1.4g saturates

5.6g fiber

26.1g sugar

>0.05g salt

Procedure:

Peel the oranges and slice into eight chunks, ensuring to remove any of the pith. Peel the bananas and slice into numerous chunks. Core and slice the apple into moderate sized pieces. Place the strawberries, banana and oranges in a bowl. Cover the fruit with yogurt and drizzle with honey. Separate into four portions and serve.

Wheat Belly Lunch Recipes

Oriental Salad

<u>Total Preparation Time:</u>

Approx 20 minutes

<u>Ingredients (serves two):</u>

1 boneless, skinless chicken breast

1 tablespoon fish sauce

Lime juice and zest

1 teaspoon of caster sugar

100g fresh baby spinach

Chopped coriander

¼ of a red onion

½ of a chili

¼ of a cucumber

<u>Nutritional Information:</u>

109 calories

19g protein

6g carbohydrates

1g fat

0g saturates

5g fiber

1.6g sugar

0g salt

Procedure:

Place the chicken in a saucepan of water. Heat until boiling and leave for 10 minutes. Drain the water from the pain and using a fork, tear the chicken into small pieces.

Combine the fish sauce, lime zest, lime juice and the sugar until you have a singular sauce.

Dice the red onion. Remove the seeds from the chili and thinly slice it. Slice the cucumber lengthways.

Slice some coriander leaves and sprinkle them over the onion, chili, chicken and cucumber.

Separate the salad into two servings, with some fish sauce to serve.

Parmesan Salad

Total Preparation Time:

Approx 20 minutes

Ingredients (serves four):

200g small mushrooms

Lemon juice

200g green beans

Mixed herbs

100g cherry tomatoes

3 tablespoons

75g parmesan

Nutritional Information:

180 calories

9g protein

3g carbohydrates

15g fat

5g saturates

2g fiber

2g sugar

0.4g salt

Procedure:

Cover the mushrooms with the lemon juice and leave for several moments.

Meanwhile, bring a saucepan of water to boil and blanch the green beans, boiling for around 5 minutes.

Combine the green beans and mushrooms in a bowl and coat with the mixed herbs, as well as a pinch of salt and pepper.

Quarter the cherry tomatoes and add to the green beans and mushrooms and drizzle the entire mixture with a little lemon juice and olive oil. Grate the parmesan into curls and mix into the salad.

Separate into two portions and serve.

Nutty Hummus

Total Preparation Time:

Approx 10 minutes

Ingredients (serves two):

380g chickpeas

Lemon zest and juice

1 tablespoon tahini

1 teaspoon smoked paprika

2 tablespoon roasted peanuts

1 teaspoon rapeseed oil

2 red apples

2 carrots

4 celery sticks

Nutritional Information:

336 calories

15g protein

35g carbohydrates

16g fat

2g saturates

13g fiber

16g sugar

0.8g salt

Procedure:

Core the red apples and slice them into moderate pieces. Peel and cut the carrots into sticks, no more than 2 inches in length. Cut the celery sticks lengthways to form long half-slices.

Combine the chickpeas with the lemon zest, lemon juice, tahini, paprika, peanuts and rapeseed oil in a food processor with a tablespoon or two of water. Process until a thick paste has formed. Serve with the carrots, celery and apple.

Greek Feta Salad

Total Preparation Time:

Approx 55 minutes

Ingredients (serves four):

4 parsnips

4 carrots

2 teaspoons of cumin seeds

400g of chickpeas

2 tablespoons of vegetable oil

500g beetroot

2 tablespoons of honey

200g hummus

2 tablespoons of white wine vinegar

200g feta cheese

Nutritional Information:

610 calories

23g protein

61g carbohydrates

26g fat

10g saturates

20g fiber

36g sugar

3.5g salt

Procedure:

Preheat the oven to gas mark 6 or 390F. Peel and cut the carrots and parsnips into sizeable chunks. In a deep tray, combine the parsnips, carrots, chickpeas and cumin seeds. Dress with olive oil and roast for half an hour, ensuring that you mix and turn over the vegetables after 15 minutes.

Dice the beetroot and cover it with honey. Add it to the tray and cook for another 10 minutes. Separate the hummus into four portions. Remove the roasted vegetables from the oven, dress with vinegar and serve with the hummus.

Pesto Salad

Total Preparation Time:

Approx 30 minutes

Ingredients (serves four):

250g broccoli

2 teaspoon rapeseed oil

3 chicken breasts

1 onion

100g watercress

175g beetroot

Basil

1 Avocado

½ a garlic clove

25g of crushed walnuts

1 tablespoon of rapeseed oil

Lemon juice and zest

Nutritional Information:

320g calories

29g protein

8g carbohydrates

18g fat

3g saturates

6g fiber

6g sugar

0.3g salt

<u>Procedure:</u>

Boil some water and blanch the broccoli. Drain the broccoli from the saucepan and run it under cold water. In a skillet, place the broccoli and drizzle it with a little rapeseed oil. Roast the broccoli in the skillet in 3 minutes sections, turning every period to enough a thorough bake. Coat the chicken with a little rapeseed oil, place it into the skillet and continue to cook for 3 minutes then turn until the chicken is white all the way through.

Chop the onions into fine slices, drizzle with lemon juice and leave on the side for several minutes.

Crush the ½ garlic clove. To make the pesto, combine the basil, avocado with the garlic, crushed walnuts and lemon juice and zest in a food processor. Add a tablespoon of water and process until a thick, oily pesto paste is produced. Separate the pesto into four serving portions.

Slice the beetroot finely into small pieces. To serve, bed four plates with watercress. Cover the watercress with broccoli, the lemon-juice covered onions, chicken and pesto.

Prawn Lunch

Total Preparation Time:

Approx 15 minutes

Ingredients (serves four):

2 packs asparagus

150g salmon fillet

8 medium cooked prawns

100g baby spinach

1 avocado

1 cucumber

¼ cup of extra virgin olive oil

1 tablespoon of lime juice

1 tablespoon red wine vinegar

1 teaspoon of brown sugar

Nutritional Information:

350g calories

15g protein

10g carbohydrates

25g fat

12g saturates

8g fiber

0g sugar

0.6g salt

Procedure:

Gently fry the asparagus over a teaspoon of olive oil for a few minutes on either side. Stone, peel and dice the avocado flesh. Slice the cucumber into chunks. Flake the salmon into pieces. Combine the asparagus, avocado, salmon, prawns and cucumber in a bowl.

Stir the remaining olive in with the lime juice, red wine vinegar and brown sugar to create a dressing.

Separate the salad into four portions and decorate with the dressing to serve.

Vegetable Soup

Total Preparation Time:

Approx. 25 minutes

Ingredients (serves four):

2 teaspoons olive oil

1 leek

500g chopped carrots

4 cups of Chicken Stock

300g chickpeas

½ teaspoon of mixed spices

5 tablespoons of natural yogurt

Chopped fresh tarragon

Nutritional Information:

180g calories

7g protein

21g carbohydrates

5g fat

1g saturates

0g fiber

11g sugar

1g salt

Procedure:

Chop the leek into thin slices. In a frying pan heat a tablespoon of olive oil and combine the chopped carrots and leek slices. Fry for 12 minutes or until the vegetables have softened.

Place the fried vegetables in a saucepan and add the chicken stock, mixed spice and chickpeas. Cover, bring to the boil and simmer for 15 minutes. Add the yogurt and tarragon.

Using a hand blender, blend the ingredients until a smooth liquidated mixture is produced. Add a pinch of salt and pepper and cook until heated. Separate into four portions and serve.

Wheat Belly Main Course Recipes

Hearty Mediterranean Stew

Total Preparation Time:

Approx 20 minutes

Ingredients (serves three):

350g pork mince

2 tablespoons olive oil

1 red onion

2 bell peppers

3 garlic cloves

1 tablespoon of smoked paprika

800g of chopped tomatoes

400g of butter beans

2 tsp of caster sugar

Parsley

Nutritional Information:

430 calories

32g protein

35g carbohydrates

15g fat

5g saturates

12g fiber

22g sugar

1.3g salt

<u>Procedure:</u>

Crush the garlic. Slice the bell peppers into thin strips and dice the red onion. Separate the mincemeat into small balls, no more than an inch in diameter. Heat the olive oil in a frying pan and gently fry the meatballs for 5 minutes. Next, add the peppers and the onion to the frying pan and continue to apply heat for another 5 minutes. Next, add the garlic and paprika and combine thoroughly. Pour the chopped tomatoes over the mixture and leave to simmer for 12 minutes. Finally, add the butter beans and leave to simmer for another twelve minutes. Serve with fresh parsley.

Filled Eggplants

Total Preparation Time:

Approx 50 minutes

Ingredients (serves four):

2 eggplants

2 tablespoons olive oil

1 onion

4 garlic cloves

A pack of cherry tomatoes

50g pitted olives

125g mozzarella

Nutritional Information:

266 calories

9g protein

14g carbohydrates

20g fat

6g saturates

5g fiber

7g sugar

1.17g salt

Procedure:

Preheat the oven to gas mark 7 or 450 degrees F. Cut the eggplants in half, lengthways. About half an inch into the eggplant, cut around the perimeter and remove the eggplant flesh within to leaving eggplant shells. Cut the flesh you remove into small pieces. Drizzle the eggplant shells with olive oil, cover them with tin foil and roast for 20 minutes.

Dice the onions. Heat some oil in a frying pan and gently fry the diced onion until lightly golden. Add the eggplant innards and continue to fry until the eggplant is entirely cooked. Add in the tomatoes and garlic, frying for a moment until the garlic is golden. Slice the olives in half and tear the mozzarella into chunks. Add the mozzarella and olives to your frying pan.

Once the eggplant shells have cooked, add the filling from the frying pan and cook for another 15 minutes. Serve with a salad or a side of your choice.

Fish Broth

Total Preparation Time:

Approx 35 minutes

Ingredients (serves two):

1 tablespoon olive oil

1 teaspoon fennel seeds

2 carrots

2 celery sticks

2 garlic cloves

2 leeks

400g chopped tomatoes

2 skinless Pollock fillets

85g shelled king prawns

Nutritional Information:

346 calories

42g protein

20g carbohydrates

8g fat

1g saturates

11g fiber

17g sugar

1.7g salt

Procedure:

Dice the carrots, celery and garlic. In a frying pan, heat some oil and add the carrots, celery, garlic, and the fennel seeds. Fry for five minutes or until the vegetables have softened. Pour in the chopped tomatoes and simmer the mixture for 20 minutes, ensuring that the frying pan is covered.

Next, chop the Pollock fillets into moderate chunks. Add the Pollock as well as the prawns into the frying pan and cook for another 3-5 minutes. Separate the meal into four portions and serve.

Mediterranean Grilled Chicken

<u>Total Preparation Time:</u>

Approx 25 minutes

<u>Ingredients (serves two):</u>

1 tablespoon rapeseed oil

Oregano

Thyme

1 teaspoon smoked paprika

½ teaspoon cayenne pepper

1 garlic clove

4 skinless, boneless chicken breasts

200g black-eyed beans

2 tomatoes

85 sweetcorn

2 spring onions

25g semi-dried tomatoes

Lime juice and zest

Coriander

1 avocado

¼ red chili

1 teaspoon olive oil

Lime juice

Nutritional Information:

491 calories

48g protein

30g carbohydrates

20g fat

4g saturates

12g fiber

10g sugar

1g salt

Procedure:

In a sealable plastic bag, combine the herbs, spices and rapeseed oil. Coat the chicken by placing it in the bag and seal. Strike the chicken to squash it slightly and leave aside for 15 minutes to marinate.

Chop the spring onions and dice the tomatoes. Combine the black-eyed beans, tomatoes, sweetcorn, spring onions, semi-dried tomatoes, lime zest, lime juice and coriander in a mixing bowl. Mix these ingredients together and set aside.

Peel, stone and remove the flesh of the avocado. Dice the avocado flesh. Remove the seeds from the chili and slice into small sections. Combine the avocado, chili, olive oil, lime juice and a little coriander and sit. Set aside this mixture for later.

Cover a grilling tray with tin foil. Under medium heat on a grill, cook the chicken, turning every 5 minutes or so to ensure an even bake. Once the chicken is golden brown and cooked in the center, remove.

Serve each chicken breast with a portion of the black-bean salad and a portion of the avocado-chili guacamole.

Spiced Salmon with Corn Salad

Total Preparation Time:

Approx 30 minutes

Ingredients (serves two):

1 garlic clove

½ teaspoon of chili powder

½ teaspoon of coriander

A pinch of ground cumin

Lime juice and zest

2 teaspoon of rapeseed oil

2 salmon fillets

1 corn on the cob

1 red onion

1 avocado

1 red pepper

1 red chilli

Sliced coriander

Nutritional Information:

530 calories

29g protein

27g carbohydrates

32g fat

5g saturates

9g fiber

12g sugar

0.2g

Procedure:

Grate the garlic into a fine dust. Place the corn into a saucepan of boiling water for 8 minutes. Remove the cob by draining the water and using a knife, scrape the corn from the cob.

Mix the chili powder, coriander and cumin with some lime juice and the garlic. Place this spice mixture in a sealable plastic bag and place the salmon within, shaking to coat. Set aside for several moments.

Dice the onion. Stone, peel and dice the avocado. Chop the red pepper into thin slices then remove the chili seeds and slice the chili. Combine the lime zest and the remaining lime juice with the onion, red pepper and chili. Add the corn.

Remove the salmon from the spice mix and fry on each side for 3 minutes.

Serve the salmon with a portion of the corn salad.

Carrot Patties

<u>Total Preparation Time:</u>

Approx 1 hour and 20 minutes

<u>Ingredients (serves four):</u>

5 carrots

400g chickpeas

Fresh, chopped coriander

2 teaspoons cumin

2 teaspoons coriander

1 medium egg

150g Greek yogurt

1 tablespoon olive oil

200g watercress

Harissa Paste

<u>Nutritional Information:</u>

260 calories

11g protein

25g carbohydrates

10g fat

3g saturates

8g fiber

14g sugar

0.6g salt

Procedure:

Peel and cut the carrots into slices. Bring a saucepan of water to the boil and add the carrots, simmering for roughly 20 minutes or until the carrots have softened. Remove the carrots add them to a mixing bowl with coriander, cumin and a beaten egg.

Mash the ingredients in the bowl and form 8 patties. Cover with cling film and leave in the fridge for at least half an hour.

Take a tablespoon of Harissa paste and dollop it over the Greek yogurt. With a spoon, stir the mixture once or twice, so a streaky pattern is formed in the yogurt.

Heat a tablespoon of olive oil and fry the patties for 3 minutes on each side. Serve with the watercress and yogurt.

GINGER STIR-FRY

<u>Total Preparation Time:</u>

Approx 25 minutes

<u>Ingredients (serves six):</u>

1 tablespoon vegetable oil

1 onion

2 garlic cloves

4cm fresh ginger

600g tofu

200g brown mushrooms

½ a cup of stir fry sauce

1 bunch of gai lan

300g three bean salad

<u>Nutritional Information:</u>

360 calories

20g protein

39g carbohydrates

13g fat

1.9g saturates

7g fiber

0g sugar

0.6g salt

Procedure:

Dice the onion and finely chop the garlic cloves. If not already prepared, cut the tofu into moderate chunks. Peel the ginger and cut it into thin strips.

Heat the vegetable oil in a wok. Fry the garlic until it is golden brown. Add the tofu to the frying pan, as well as the ginger. Fry for 3 and ½ minutes.

Next add the mushrooms and stir-fry sauce to the mix. Fry for 3 minutes and then add the gai lan. Stir fry until the gai lan has softened, which should only take a moment. Add the three beans and fry for another 3 minutes.

Separate into six portions and serve.

THE 21 DAY MEAL PLAN

The previous three chapters contained seven recipes for each meal of the day. This provides a useful framework to construct a meal plan – for this eBook we will use these recipes to provide a 21 day meal plan, with enough variety so that you do not get bored. However, feel free to mix and match the recipes as you please; the following arrangement is just a suggestion.

Also, be aware of the nature of wheat belly diet. It is not by its nature, a calorie controlled diet. If you feel hungry, do not feel as if you cannot snack throughout the day. For the following meal plan between breakfast and lunch as well as between lunch and dinner it is suggested that you snack. However, if you do not feel hungry, then simply pass on this opportunity. Likewise some of the meals provided are lower in calorie count than others – for the meals that are especially low, consider having a greater serving. Ultimately, adjust this meal plan to your own needs.

Good snacks include fruit, nuts and seeds. Avoid processed goods, especially wheat-based goods at all costs. The recipes in this book have also avoided most carbohydrates that the wheat-belly diet suggests you avoid such as potatoes. If you wish to add these to your diet do it sparingly – use them as you might use a 'treat' in another diet.

Without any further ado, here is the meal plan:

WEEK 1

Monday:

Breakfast: Strawberry Smoothie

Snack 1

Lunch: Oriental Salad

Snack 2

Dinner: Filled Eggplants

Tuesday:

Breakfast: Asparagus & Eggs

Snack 1

Lunch: Parmesan Salad

Snack 2

Dinner: Fish Broth

Wednesday:

Breakfast: Orange & Date Salad

Snack 1

Lunch: Nutty hummus

Snack 2

Dinner: Mediterranean Grilled Chicken

Thursday:

Breakfast: Scrambled Eggs

Snack 1

Lunch: Greek feta Salad

Snack 2

Dinner: Spiced Salmon with Corn Salad

Friday

Breakfast: Egg pots

Snack 1

Lunch: Pesto Salad

Snack 2

Dinner: Carrot Patties

Saturday:

Breakfast: Exotic Breakfast Smoothie

Snack 1

Lunch: Prawn Lunch

Snack 2

Dinner: Ginger stir-fry

Sunday:

Breakfast: Fruit Salad

Snack 1

Lunch: Vegetable Soup

Snack 2

Dinner: Hearty Mediterranean Stew

Week 2

Monday:

Breakfast: Fruit Salad

Snack 1

Lunch: Pesto Salad

Snack 2

Dinner: Mediterranean Grilled Chicken

Tuesday:

Breakfast: Egg Pots

Snack 1

Lunch: Nutty hummus

Snack 2

Dinner: Filled Eggplants

Wednesday:

Breakfast: Orange & Date Salad

Snack 1

Lunch: Oriental Salad

Snack 2

Dinner: Ginger stir-fry

Thursday:

Breakfast: Strawberry Smoothie

Snack 1

Lunch: Prawn Lunch

Snack 2

Dinner: Spiced Salmon with Corn Salad

Friday

Breakfast: Exotic Breakfast Smoothie

Snack 1

Lunch: Greek Feta Salad

Snack 2

Dinner: Fish Broth

Saturday:

Breakfast: Scrambled Eggs

Snack 1

Lunch: Parmesan Salad

Snack 2

Dinner: Hearty Mediterranean Stew

Sunday:

Breakfast: Asparagus & Eggs

Snack 1

Lunch: Vegetable Soup

Snack 2

Dinner: Carrot Patties

Week 3

Monday:

Breakfast*:* Exotic Fruit Smoothie

Snack 1

Lunch*:* Parmesan Salad

Snack 2

Dinner*:* Mediterranean Grilled Chicken

Tuesday:

Breakfast*:* Orange & Date Salad

Snack 1

Lunch*:* Prawn Lunch

Snack 2

Dinner*:* Hearty Mediterranean Stew

Wednesday:

Breakfast*:* Fruit Salad

Snack 1

Lunch*:* Nutty hummus

Snack 2

Dinner*:* Spiced Salmon with Corn Salad

Thursday:

Breakfast: Asparagus & Eggs

Snack 1

Lunch: Vegetable Soup

Snack 2

Dinner: Ginger stir-fry

Friday

Breakfast: Scrambled Eggs

Snack 1

Lunch: Oriental Salad

Snack 2

Dinner: Filled Eggplants

Saturday:

Breakfast: Strawberry Smoothie

Snack 1

Lunch: Pesto Salad

Snack 2

Dinner: Carrot Patties

Sunday:

Breakfast: Egg Pots

Snack 1

Lunch: Greek Feta Salad

Snack 2

Dinner: Fish Broth

Complete Food List

This complete food list has everything you need to make all of the recipes in this book. It has been provided to make shopping for these recipes easier. I do hope you find it helpful!

Fruits
Avocado
Strawberries
Lemons
Oranges
Dates
Mango
Bananas
Apples
Limes
Cherry Tomatoes
Tomatoes

Vegetables
Asparagus
Spinach
Baby Spinach
Red Onion
Cucumber
Small Mushrooms
Green Beans
Chickpeas
Carrots
Celery
Parsnips
Beetroot
Broccoli
Watercress
Garlic cloves

Leeks
Bell Peppers
Butter beans
Pitted Olives
Black eyed beans
Sweetcorn
Spring Onions
Corn of the cob
Three Bean Salad
Gai Lan

Sauces, Oils & Condiments
Hummus
Honey
Olive Oil
Chilli Powder
Paprika
Mint Leaves
Rose Syrup
Fish Sauce
Caster Sugar
Mixed Herbs
Tahini
Smoked Paprika
Rapeseed Oil
Cumin Seeds
Vegetable Oil
White Whine Vinegar
Watercress
Basil
Garlic Cloves
Red wine vinegar
Brown sugar
Chicken stock
Mixed Spice
Fresh Tarragon

Parsley
Fennel Seeds
Oregano
Thyme
Cayenne Pepper
Harissa paste
Fresh ginger
Stir Fry Sauce

Dairy, Cheeses, Fishes & Meats
Natural Yogurt
Eggs
Cream
Butter
Skimmed Milk
Parmesan
Feta Cheese
Chicken Breast
Salmon fillet
Crooked Prawns
Pork mincemeat
Mozzarella
Pollock Fillets

Nuts & Seeds
Almond Meal
Almonds
Walnuts

Others
Tofu
Ice

Conclusion

Conventional diets are notoriously hard. There is no shortcut or workaround to losing weight. However, you do not need to make the process of weight loss more difficult it than it needs to be by embracing harsh and taxing diets such as calorie counting or extraordinary fad regimes. The wheat belly diet offers a practical solution – no weird or difficult restrictions, and no calorie counting. The only and single demand it places is that you avoid wheat, wheat-based products and a few other grains and carbohydrates.

The challenge of eating a diet within the wheat belly limitations can seem daunting because of how ubiquitous wheat and wheat-based products have penetrated into our dietary habits. When we actually look on the label, it seems most foods we eat contain copious amounts of wheat. In spite of this, once you begin to explore and investigate your dietary habits just a little bit further you realize there is a wealth of recipes and foods still available. It's just that before you realized how much wheat you are consuming, you were not looking for alternatives.

This eBook has provided you with dozens of recipes, allowing you to cook healthy and tasty, wheat belly meals for every meal of the day. Furthermore, this eBook has also provided you with these recipes ordered into a handy meal plan to get your new diet off the ground.

Now it is up to you; you have been informed about all the disadvantages of a regular diet, with its overdose of wheat and other grains. You have also been given all the tools you need to avoid this diet, lose weight, and improve your blood sugar, energy levels as well as digestive health. It is your decision to follow a particular diet, but now with the help of this eBook, you can make the right choice.

About the Author

I am a mother to three beautiful children and a wife to a wonderful husband. I have a passion to teach others and can often be found volunteering in my local community.

During college I worked within my family catering business to support myself. After graduating I opened a chain of small cafes that I ran successfully for a number of years. Now whilst being a stay at home mom, I am able share my skills, knowledge and experience through my books. I feel a great deal of satisfaction when helping others and seeing them flourish to their maximum potential.

Please check out my author page on Amazon to see my latest publications. Please don't forget to **join my Book Club** for a free books, newsletters and updates.

Once again I want to thank you for reading my book. I really hope you got a lot out of it.

If you enjoyed this book I would really appreciate it if you could leave me a positive review on Amazon. You can **click here** to go directly to the book on Amazon and leave your review.

I love getting feedback from my readers and reviews on Amazon really do make a difference. I read all my reviews and would really appreciate your thoughts.

Thanks so much.
CHARLOTTE MOYER

Other Books By Author

Wheat Belly: 31 Delicious Wheat Free Recipes to Lose Weight Fast

Vegan: 35 High Protein Vegan Recipes for Weight Loss and Building Muscle

How to Bake Perfectly: 101 Tips, Tricks & Cheats for Baking Recipes

How to Make Money from Home: 7 Steps to Make Money from Baking recipes

ALL RIGHTS RESERVED. No part of this publication may be reproduced or transmitted in any form whatsoever, electronic, or mechanical, including photocopying, recording, or by any informational storage or retrieval system without express written, dated and signed permission from the author.

CC Licence; Pictures

Made in the USA
Middletown, DE
06 November 2015